NIGHT
LIGHTNING

JULIA CASTERTON

NIGHT LIGHTNING

**A MEMORIAL COLLECTION EDITED BY
JUDY GAHAGAN AND MARTINA EVANS**

The Rialto

ACKNOWLEDGEMENTS

Some of these poems first appeared in *Ambit* and in *The Rialto*. Others may have appeared in other magazines and we apologise to editors where attribution has not been possible.

Special thanks to Chris Nawrat for granting access to Julia's files and for all his help in making this collection possible.

First Published in 2007

The Rialto, PO Box 309, Aylsham, Norwich, England NR11 6LN

© The Estate of Julia Casterton.

ISBN 978-0-9551273-1-1

The publisher acknowledges financial assistance from the Arts Council of England, East.

The Rialto is a Registered Charity No. 297553

Typeset in Berling Roman 10pt on 13pt leading

Design and artwork by Starfish, Norwich.

Cover image Villám by Dénes Péter Horváth

Back cover image: Julia at Aldeburgh 2005 © The Poetry Trust
Photographer: Peter Everard Smith.

Printed by Micropress Limited, Halesworth, Suffolk.

Thank you Julia

CONTENTS

EARLY POEMS

NEW POEMS

FOREWORD

Through Julia's work as poet, editor and teacher there ran a common shining thread – that of her remarkable character. To all these domains she brought lightness, enthusiasm, intense involvement, vast cultural reach and an acute critical judgement. Her earliest work appeared in the early 80s in *Ambit* magazine where she was to later join the editorial team. She loved the work of Edwin Brock who was then poetry editor. She was a charismatic presence at *Ambit* readings and celebrations – to which she'd cycle miles, baskets loaded with magazines. Her welcoming presence to everyone at those events is unforgettable.

Her teaching offered a counterpoint of developing ideas and aesthetic criteria to her own writing. She was an extraordinary teacher and her commitment to every student's work contributed to a heritage and a great following. In teaching her first response was enthusiasm, a probing to understand a student's preoccupation and only (but always) at a later stage, a searching critique of the work under scrutiny.

Certain personal themes emerge in her work – from the early pamphlets like *Troublesome Cattle* (with Liz Cashdun) and *That Slut Cleopatra*, the myriad poems published in journals, through the wonderful prize-winning Rialto collection *The Doves of Finistere* to the present posthumous collection *Night Lightning*. Those themes range from the energy and fun of one of her first *Ambit* poems: 'Oh you Giglets/you gorgeous gaping girls/playground-striped' to the intense spirituality and revelation of private suffering that was always concealed from other people. The freedom and risk in this present collection open doors to any poet searching for the potential scope of a poetic canon.

Martin Bax and Judy Gahagan

FISHING WITH ALEJANDRE

We sit on the café terrace together, Alejandre and I,
eating navacas, razor shell clams, opening the bivalve,
tasting salt and the sea wrack, with its cream, its foam.

Alejandre gathers them from the waters of the ria in the summer.
I see him, shaking with cold in his wet-suit after hours under water,
with his bag of mother of pearl knives, his shiny razor shells.

In the winter, in the mal tiempo, he writes poems.
I ask him why the lines are longer here.
Ten syllables in English is the norm, twelve in French.

Why fourteen in Gallego?
Because of the verbs, he tells me. Our verbs are longer.

I ease out the clam's long muscle of meat,
its long tongue of sweetness.
We continue to eat.

SENOR LOBELINOS

We sit over his nets. He doesn't fish now, but sometimes he sits with the nets
in the fishermen's house on the lonxa. Somehow we talk a little,
me with my small Gallego, he with his small English, among the nets.

The fishermen leave for the fish, he says. They take the currents they've
always taken,
to the New World, for the cod, for the hake. The secret routes, sailed by
the Basques, the Gallegans, long before Columbus. And sometimes they make
another life, away from the rain of Galicia, leaving their families on the
calle des emigrantes, for a softer life away from here.

But he has not done this. He always returned with his catch
and now his daughter is a lawyer in Santiago, his wife is round and happy.

I ask him what was his best moment, in his life with the fish,
and he says in Canada. He heard his own name spoken
by an old man in a bar. It was his grandfather in a corner chair.
The whole afternoon they were together. That was when
he knew that the bitter season means nothing, because although the sea
draws us out and we are scattered, there is a magnet at the root of the world
brings us together face to face.

THE GARDENER

He leaves the house wreathed in shouting,
sheathed with the morning he is trying to put on.
Her voice from the kitchen, Come Back, COME BACK.
But he can't bear it, he has to go, to the kidney bean stakes,
                                        the flowering potato plants,
away from her. He struggles through the door with his love,
his hoe and his rake, down the path,
beating through her stings with his trowel, his face bent against her,
the path a wind, a silk road that smells of vanilla.
Path that is no path, leading east, the way the stories go.

He is Yusuf, the Lord's beloved, and she Zuleika,
cheeks etched with tears, hair white, eyes blind with love for him.

What can he do with her terrible wants?
He puts them in the ground with weeds and hacks them off at the roots.
He can feel them deflecting, a swan settling its feathers on the river,
something resolving into a cloud by his head.

It is the summer's second season of blackberries
                        and as his hand bleeds over thorns
he can live again, even with the schisms that lie between them,
the slate faults in the mountain that will neither open nor close.

He is a minute reproductive body, characteristic of flowerless plants.
Only the wind can help him. He digs himself down with her wants,
not knowing his own, investing them together in the garden.
The wind is very high, his spores are everywhere.

Is there somewhere they can go, some wilderness where menstrual blood
sits on the tongue like honey, and the calluses on his fingers soften,
as he touches her in the language she knows?

She may approach him by the garden's margins,
air stained blue by flowers. He may hold out his hand to her,
startled at such a visit in the morning, as if a silver fox had come,
and might disappear at any moment through the door in the privet
hedge.
She may take his hand that is offered, he may lead her to a plant
whose name he does not know, and she may tell it.
Or she may be ignorant also, and they stand and look at
                                        the plant without speaking.
They may not be perturbed by what they do not know.

THE GAMBLE

'We have seen in deeds, not in words, what the brotherhood of the sea means.' – Sergei Ivanov in The Guardian, *Monday August 8th 2005, thanking the British navy for cutting his submarine free.*

It seems like a dead end. The cutting device
that can slice through steel cable half a metre thick
can't reach the final rope.
Even the Scorpio's robotic arms can't push the submarine up.

The last obstacle appears to have it trapped.
Air will run out by midday.
So they take a gamble,
filling the submarine's ballast tanks with air from its reserves.

You can only do this once.
Twice, and the whole crew dies in a suffocation of ice.

They wait.

And in a flurry of bubbles, plankton, seabed dust,
fragments of fishing net, the submarine rises up,
disappearing off the team's monitors,
out of sight of the cameras.

A cry in Russian breaks the silence
as it surfaces on the other side of the ship
and the captain leads his men ashore.
The one thing needed in the end was air.

MEN WITH STAINED TEETH WHO SPIN YOU

I was out at the fair with my friends. Whitsuntide. Wakes Week,
and he was there like before on the waltzer, like thirty years before.

Same hair, same raddled mouth, black teeth,
same I'm-gonna-spin-you-till-you're-stupid eyes.

Only now, he could be my son.
But he's going to spin me all the same.

I never knew that I could scream like this,
my body a missile cruising close to the earth,

pulled from all directions by the core,
hurting no one, but something breaking inside, that wants to be broken

by the greater gravity here, as if I were on a larger planet,
G force blessing all around me.

Even his lumpish Have-you-had-enough-yet, or-do-you-want-some-more?
sounds sweet at this late stage. As though I were still invulnerable,

as though girls didn't die at the hands of fairgroundmen.
Alighting, I say, Thank-you, that-was-very-good,

as I did in the old days. And when I get out of the bath the next morning,
on my left thigh is the magnificent, predictable, huge black bruise.

THE LISTENING CHOIR

Very very tired. I've told my story
and I am gone. The infant self
that lives in stories, the hungry, guzzling self,
is satisfied. And now there's space
for all the other selves were never listened to.

Room's hotting up, lit by the floating headlamps
from dumb dyslexic ancient mariners,
dysphasic mouths, all would-be guzzlers
shut up before they got a word in.

World – full of would-be mouths,
would-be tongues, yelling their stories to a
would-be dolorosa too full of her own
to lend an ear. They drift up now

from the sea-mulch of this bed,
where sleep has another quality
than pure refreshment, where they are duties
not heard-of by walls or washing-powder.

There, in the sea-mulch:
man with red eyes, who cannot sleep
for the damage done to this back. He eyes me,
spineless, suspicious, from his world of forced labour;

young man rich from telecommunications,
then poor from yet another crash.
His street-living. His heart-failures.
Stories pour. Who'd have thought

the young men had so much blood in them?
When one story is told, the teller
grows ears. He cannot hear till then.
The world has ears and we are many.

A lot of work. The sleepers listen in their sleep.
Sometimes we cover our ears, but stories must get worse
before any good can come of them.
Sometimes we faint, but there is no escape.

Every story left unturned must be turned
again. Not hearing is a false economy.
Each telling makes for more exaggeration.
If you want a clear narrative, hear it quickly.

Christ come quickly. Like death,
we have to get it over with.
Then the pain of the refiner's fire.
Then the invitation to the listening choir.

NIGHT LIGHTNING

All night it's been flapping past my balcony in sheets
of dull green, dull blue, dull orange, dirty white.

It's lightning, but these are not the skybolts,
the flashes of glory from some fearsome god.

These are dumplings of soiled linen,
Bedsheets of an old lout.

And they keep coming. I ask my step-mother over the phone
What are they?

She says it's night lightning. When the corn
Hasn't had enough sun, night lightning comes to ripen it.

It's nature's way of making ripe
corn that would be green or rotten.

You'll be needing it too, she says.
Stand on your rooftop. Let it ripen you.

EXPENSIVE

Each time I come here I am worn out,
slumping in the doorway
between where this world thins
and the other peeps through.

I hear a family through the wall
where no family is
and in the easy chair
someone fades into pre-existence

as I enter the room.
I must make peace with the place
and cease treating it
as just another fishing town.

Everywhere the birth-rate falls,
yet here children are born
like sociable dogs, in packs.
The locals measure their steps

while I am on the verge of expiry.
What will it take, to quieten down,
so I can cease being beaten out like copper
and be pink and sturdy as the African daisies

arraying themselves nightly in the dunes?

END OF THE HOLIDAY

Sun turning to old drinkwater, beach empty,
or full, rather, of its old inhabitants.
Sandpipers, gulls, the first silent
on their little legs, the second
a late-August symphony of complaint
above the silvery baby shoals that now run
more alive in a stream that's opening slowly
over an unwatched mystery of glowing sand.

The tide's turned and tipped the year over
into its own shadow. The sun, overworked,
is taking a holiday. There's a bedding-down
of skin, comfort. A wound has closed.
Contempt for the hysteria of summer falls away.
I drink my fill of what was there before.

IF

What if, instead of bracing ourselves against the wind
we just let go and let the currents take us?

Our bones would get used to it in the end,
we'd go beyond the usual human diseases

where we fight against ourselves, auto-immune,
and learn the joy of giving in to its windy graces.

Lift! You'd feel your armpits stretch and thicken,
the cool beneath, the vast world empty of desires

just waiting
for you to let it be yours.

The birds won't mind.
There are still just enough trees

for those who need a branch for the night to have one.
The fearful can return to their houses

if they want,
until it dawns on them that the universe

is theirs to swoop about in.
Everywhere is your house.

You don't need your feet on the ground
because now the wind has freed you

there are no stakes anymore saying This Is Mine.
No mortgages.

You're flying with your hollow bones
beyond gravity

which was just something we assumed, a convention
that held us down until we leaned into the upward drifts.

THE DAY HIDES

It's true that when the day comes out in her full glory
she's too much for me.

Something hurts inside. I want to respond
to all that fiery kindness, and I can't.

When I watched the moon set
early this morning, red-gold and full of herself,

I paled, up in my high kitchen.
How could I compete, or even be there alongside

a day like this one coming?
So when she hid herself a little

behind long flowing clouds,
I thought Now I Can Cope

and stepped out bravely into her
to buy bread.

MOON ON THE KITCHEN FLOOR

Each time I rise in the darkness, the pattern of light's different.
The bed is warm as new-laid yellow yolk
but the cold kitchen floor keeps changing,

flooding itself with a bluey whiteness
beyond the sad orange of the streetlamps.
Look Out! I remember your voice calling

when I was humping round the vacuum cleaner.
You call again now, out of my dream –

Look Out! The moonstars are out!

I look up from the floor that shines up at me,
a shifting bed of blueness,
and there she is again, your moon,

so bright it's hard to look,
but I do, because her light's so confident,
as if she's forgotten anyone ever walked on her,

making me remember how she saved us
from my anger at the cleaning
and could save us again

if we could just look up
and see that we are here,
still under her,

and that whatever we did, she still shone.

ANGELS

I never turn a corner but I see an angel
sleeping in the crook of a pear tree's double trunk,
encrypted in the slippery rainbow membrane of an onion.
How many angels on a pinhead? There is no limit,
and no limit either in the sliding slimness of the pin.

Angels have even found a way of entering
the flat banality of synthetics. I find them
in plastic, in the swishing folds of viscose,
their chromatic joy sing-shining in the cellular structure
of every hideous knick-knack.

They are shimmering in perspex,
capsules, the little yellow pills I have to take each day –
and especially in the pharmacist's shy face
as he advises 'Take they with water.
And space them out if you feel a little nausea.'

THE FLOWER SHIPS
after Chateaubriand

Though you are decked for sacrifice, bound to a tree of tears and sleep
in the wood of blood, the torches lighted, the night waxing on,
your courage is not soft. Though your tired eyes are closed
in the heavy sleep of the wretched, the sensation so strong
that you are about to cry out, a hand covers your mouth
and a voice you recognise tells you to be quiet. The middle current
sweeps the dead pines and oaks to the sea, and on the side current,
floating islands of water lilies, pinkish yellow flames, rise like little banners.
Blue herons, green snakes, young crocodiles, and somehow, you also,
sail as passengers on the flower ships, and the colony, unfolding its sails
to the wind, drifts into some hidden bend of the river.

IN THE BLOOD WARD

We are all empty, some of us a little dizzy
but our doctors fill us up with blood

so we can be busy
once again, so we can go to work for our lord,

do things in the noisy
world, live with a calm head,

and thoughts not fizzy
anymore with this music from abroad

that our expressions, longings, easy
breathing, admit we've overheard.

               Why the secrecy?
Silence always seems to be the word,

because if it knew of this conspiracy,
the world would keep us still more occupied,

deaf to the drowsy
pipes we heard from somewhere in the reeds

when we were getting really hazy
from the loss of blood.

SATI'S BATIK SHAWL
(JUAN CANALEJO HOSPITAL, LA CORUNA)

has charmed the night away again. Maroon, yellow and cream, loose-woven,
I tie it round my eyes while hell breaks loose.

They're in and out all the time, these ladies with the lamp,
in a language I can't quite follow. So I wrap it round my eyes.

Why not be blind as well as dumb? Give ignorance my full surrender
under the loose-woven shawl that Sati brought to me from India.

TRAVELS WITH OUR GHOSTS

When I close my eyes she is there, clothed in the software of the dead,
their uranium comfort. She bends over a picture of herself
and she is still there when my dream has ended.

On other nights I live with a man I haven't seen for twenty years,
since before the birth of my second child. We walk by a lake,
and I rest in his golden railway carriage. He comes to me
when others leave. He's missing a tooth. I visit him in dreams,
his house by water, or a houseboat on water. I have a life with him.

My second child, immunized by the winds of Chernobyl, holds Russian ghosts
in venom doses in her white blood cells, provoking the reds to action
if a Pikey picks on her dark-skinned friend. As the Pikey carries ghosts
of Levellers inside his heart, their push for fairness twisted on our broken streets,
pikes slivered into sharps.

                    And you, my dear, who tell me
never to go back. What if you too live in the dreams
of women who once knew you? What if your ghost is some nights
at work near Inverness, giving comfort to a woman from before,
even before you're dead?

                    Would you be so cocksure
that this is all there is, this newsprint, these paltry images,
if you could see the satisfaction in her face after you'd visited?

EARLY AUTUMN MANOEUVRES

This is when green leaves become heroic,
hanging or standing so still on the sycamores,

the palm trees or the birches, as if autumn
won't notice them if they play dead

in the uncanny grey static of the warm October air.
And the petunias, begonias, the lavender lanterns

beam themselves out, riotous assemblies of peaches, pinks,
lilacs and terrifying whites, to frighten the winter,

or overwhelm it with love, make it submit
to colour going on and on without relent.

The lilies that my sister put in a high glass vase in my room
ease out their pinkness into a lolling, lazy yellow,

sliding their scent into my daytime reading, secreting
the imperial army of their perfume,

a Stalingrad without starvation,
making the adversary drunk on divine exhalations

with no opinion whatever
of time, or the dying year.

THE CROWDED GENIUS OF STANDARD ROSETREES IN GRAVEYARDS

It goes without saying that we are rosetrees once we tip over,
or birds, nodding and flopping in our early flights,

surprised by our own fledging, an unconceived rain of younger happiness,
the cleverness of our own footfalls, invisible as the breathing of flowers

around our erstwhile feet, breathing themselves
out of what was so recently ourselves, a thicker element.

How will we live in our bird-selves, our flower-selves?
Quickly, easily, every mistake the next becoming.

THE RESTORED EDITION

They said the book was lost, drowned,
but yesterday I met a woman who'd learned
the art of restoring damaged books from firemen.

I asked her why she was drawn to this work.
Was it the earthquake in California?
Was it living on the fault-line?

No, it was her brother. He's burned down
their house. She'd started thinking then, at ten,
how you can save some things, or bring them back.

She restored the books when a fire happened
at a big library, the files from Piper Alpha,
the oil-rig an upside-down coffin

of drowned workmen. Now she's come to me
because she couldn't write. I said
I too had lost a book, and she replied

It's there, you'll have to go to the forest
to find it. It's partly eaten by ants,
but not all the words are gone.

How do I put it back together?
That's how you'll find it, she said.

Putting it back together. Mine's there too.

It was in an old computer, locked in a dirty back room.
A computer torture-chamber of a room.

I pulled it out and found a printer,
hardly breathing for the weight
but it was there all right,

the only thing on the disc in English.
But not a tongue I knew.
I had to learn another language

from birth, and then translate.

UNTITLED PROSE POEMS

1.
I have cut a branch from the blossoming almond tree. The green wood didn't want to light, but I protested, and when it burst into flame, slow, curling flame, blue and orange on the shingle where I had lain it, I walked around it slowly, in my own slow fire, murmuring your name… Kleis, Kleis, return. Wind, wind, carry the love-longing to my daughter wherever she might be. Sea, carry me over to the den of my daughter. Moon, shed your beams on the den of my daughter. Let her be revealed to me. Kleis, Kleis, return. The almond blossoms burst into tiny fires one by one. As they flamed and gave up their light, I made them into little tongues of fire, singing to her, calling to her with my voice – Kleis, Kleis, return. Wherever you may be, however fierce your fury, let it down in bursts of flaming blossom. Kleis, come to Mitylene. Come back to me.

2.
Because you do not come to me in days, you come to me in dreams. You wait in hallways saying that all your money's been stolen. What can this mean? I wait for night, a supplicant on the temple steps, shaded by gingkos. I wait for night, for darkness, for the young avatar to come out, the one who knows everything, who knows about repair, and pity. Who brings a glimpse of you to me, for pity, in the night.

3.
At last I remember your dreams of flying, the dreams you recounted with such happiness the mornings after they came to you. At first you could just skip a little higher and for a little longer than usual. Then you began to direct your flights. When you were higher in the air you saw a man hovering in a tree giving you encouragement, and an old woman, terse and grumpy, who made it clear that you had to fly or you would stop living your life. So you flew, Kleis, you flew.

4.

A wind batters all my houses now. I try to hold on but everything
slides around. I believe that a woman has called up a wind to uproot
me, and all I can do is learn to enter the world of the wind, to live
inside my rejected elements. But all my steps are broken.

5.

When I look out to sea, the salt water is sandy-coloured and it merges
with the sky in peach and fawn. Is this merging one of your reasons
for leaving? That you had to carry yourself across the skypath so you
could become who you are? I remember when you were a child how
dismally you walked away from me, how you had your own work to
do before you even understood what work might be.

6.

On these cool sunny days there is even a joy in waiting. Any tall girl
walking down the sand could be you, until she gets closer. Which is
why I stay in one place and do not move.

7.

Then I thought of all the places I myself had lived – in a palace, a
room in the clouds, a fisherman's hut, a wooden shed in the forest.
And how they all live together now, all my dwelling-places, within the
basilica of my own mind, and I can remember them with love because
they housed me until I had to leave them. Will you remember
Mitylene, Kleis? Was it home for you while you lived here?

8.

I am tired in my limbs. Wine does me no good, I keep leaning back.
The wind outside is higher even than yesterday. I'd like to rest but
the small lemon tree blew down this morning and I wonder will I
build it a heavy pot? Perhaps I could bake a coiled container
in a pit in the sand. My fingernails are dirty and I'm putting off
washing them until I've written you this short but troubled letter.
Where shall I send it? Shall I plant it with the lemon tree in the
coilpot I am building?

9.

My body is my house. It is the only place I can live, just as air is all I have to breathe. I can let my body rest. Even this writing causes me to sit still. There is no reason to be afraid. No one wants to kill me, not even you, Kleis, who winded me so badly that for a while I could find no air to breathe. As if there was nowhere I could live, and my body was no longer my own house.

10.

Today I saw my own mother, now long dead, sitting begging in the porch of our basilica. Her snake eyes tracked me as I approached her. Why are you begging, I demanded. It is the afterlife, surely you have enough. We bring our debts with us, she told me. When I was alive I gave you more than I had. Here we live on our wealth, not on what we squandered. Most of us are beggars here. I came searching for you, Kleis, and all I find is my own mother and another old woman.

11.

The sea beneath my window has been churned by the moon and the wind, and the myrtle bushes are churning too. It is all trying to get into my little house, along the moonpath of the sea. Is this the path you walked away on? I pictured you riding with Hades, but you left knowingly, taking every keepsake, even your father's sleeping-bag, so there is nothing here with which I can conjure you back.

12.

But unrequited love is everywhere. Planets that breathe pure love on me so I may breathe, trees darkened by no civilisation but our own, a lung of land across my island, looping in ecstasy around the shifting plates of the world. And all I do is root it up (I don't need this, or this), and all the time the longing for what I cannot have. When the blackbird has just flown low across my garden, and the cyclamen, colour of my mother's nuptials, forms and re-forms its implacable velvet love, rolling over and over, and I've only just seen it, ointment that was always already there, washing my feet.

13.
I stand on oxygen that happens to be called rock, stroked by lightning from our first firewell. Storm chasers compete for the incandescence, our moon splashed out of this planet, her eyelids reinforced by bone, on a lost journey. Musk oxen are animals, dragon doctors claim to cure anything, and the male spider spins a bridal veil to hold his bride still. The moon splashes out, animals compete to be storms on the moon, that holds a cure for this planet that we happen to call a bride, a cure for her eyelids, stroked by the first firewell of the oxen. I wait on the rock for her fingers to be reinforced, to be stormed, by the oxygen of animals, for lightning, incandescent dragon-musk to veil my eyelids, for the moon in her bridal splashing.

14.
How dark it is today. The sea is a sandy greyness and I know that the boats I can see on the thin line of the horizon will bring me nothing. I have to think. Only in my mind will I discover what has become of you.

15.
As night comes on I imagine that the heaving waves that wash so near my wooden house are whales, their round backs rolling towards me for company. But anything is company on the good days, when gratitude pours out of me as tears. On the bad I sit dry-eyed and stare at the whaleless sea and wait for news of you.

16.
I met myself as an old woman in a dream last night. She was rough with me, taking me by the sleeve, saying what was I about, complaining about my life, my lack of life, when all I had to do was take life by the sleeve and be rough with it. Because if you are not rough with life it will be rough with you she said, giving me a rough shake.

17.
It's the shortest day. There's a flower in the cold on a stalk of light, whose burning, white-hot bloom holds winter, wrapped and mossed deep down, in a freezing cup of growth. The flower is hidden, but the heat from its veins pours outwards, a slow but shining creature that moves with its own surpassing grace, warm to me beneath its perfect boundary of ice as I stretch out my hand.

18.
In a daydream of late afternoon, the lights of my dream coming on as the dark descended, I saw Paris offering his apple. Hera and Athene hardly figured at all, only as two round stones to add seriousness to the beach, and Aphrodite sat cross-legged in the middle distance, dishevelled, taking no notice of him. It's yours, he seemed to say. Of all the women, even the Queen of Heaven, you are the one. But she wasn't looking. Surely his arms will get tired I thought. Surely he'll say, Do you want this apple or not? But still he stood. Perhaps she replied, Well, just one. I've so many at home in boxes, I don't really need... But if it will help you out. You see, I AM love.

19.
There are dreams that I can feel running away from me on waking. Some dreams stay, and others return to their own dark home, just as some flowers seem to emit light, illuminating the night with their own energy, while others emit darkness, gathering the day into rest, relieving, with their shade, the day of itself.

20.
Does pain remember us once it has left? Pierced with deep knives, we may cry out, but once a careful nurse removes them, our limbs stretch, back in the lucent being of our own presence. Does pain miss the body it once possessed, hovering in the air with no home? Where does it live once it has left us? Should we build it a warm house so it will not be homeless and covet ours?

HERON

Some thing is swaying towards me
across the pond, along the island.
Something grey, rickety,
a mad anorexic flashed with blue.

Across the pond, along the island,
an anorexic maybe, hungry governess
or a governor's slave, swaying
lifting knock-kneed legs one by one,

Something grey, rickety,
and surely it is very hungry,
stretching what could be its neck
from what I take is its throat.

A mad anorexic flashed with blue,
wearing what could be a crown.
Crowned with some kind of grace,
some island grace, some grey and hungry island grace.

An anorexic maybe, hungry governess.
But look at its neck, and look at
what surely now must be a throat.
Now it turns, I see it must be so –

Or a governor's slave, swaying
in all the penalties of loss.
Bowing, bending to display
the throat that was once his own.

Lifting the knock-kneed legs one by one
to ease the pain of creatureness
in a body owned by someone,
someone else.

Something grey, rickety –
at least it seems so.
But when it turns on seeming hopeless legs
I see it from another side.

And surely it is very hungry –
but look! Look at its throat,
the way the perfect snake of neck
bends into breast. And the breast –

Stretching what could be neck – is neck –
planted in pure heron breast. Enormous wings,
spread wide, and crowned with grace,
a grey and hungry kind of island grace.

INSIDE THE SEQUOIA

I think we may have got it wrong.
The point is, surely, to keep on like this
for two thousand years,
remember in the brittle, massive, tannin bark
the time we talked with Our Lady,
not sell it for security.

Only fire can make it come.
Bears, timberwolves, the forest floor,
spongy, thick, will not help.
It's the fire, doleful,
a habitat clearing its throat,
compels it to happen.

And it won't stop. It keeps
making itself, too big,
too big for anything,
the length of a religion.
Men can live in it.
I crawl in it now

through the fissure on my hands and knees,
Sequoia dust in my mouth,
arms that could not hold a thousandth part
of what held weather, genocide and gold
without a word. Quiet. Be quiet.

WATER CREED

I believe in water.
I believe that I will hear it running –

I believe that I will see the coot
the hunchbacked moorhen
on one leg by their nests

in running water.
That when I sit by the river
I will see the water rat plough his way

across the surface, his ginger fur
wet and ruffled
through the brown water.

That when I listen
I will hear the friction and the creak
of swan's wings

as they lift themselves up, the noise
and the strain of their rising.
And then, after many circles,

the rush of broad feet as they
land on water, pushing it all outwards
filling the river with their warm white bodies.

ICE RINK

The other skaters make a strobe.
I watch my girls shine
and flicker through them
skinny, wobbling

rock and reggae
press the ice's edge.

In my winter coat I watch –
they are hardly clothed
red tights and bits
of pink and purple

drifts of cold air
pile outwards round my fingers

they are weaving a path
through the bodies
arms haywire
       like puppets
they've not quite got it

and it's this that grips me
more than the cold;
the brave unskilful way
they break a path
through ice
      air
      the crowd
– or does the world just open for them?

My eyes are out like hat-pegs.
Such little girls
          raw shrimps
anyone could steal them
a flash of red on the ice
and I relax.

There they are!
          Skating the earth's edge
bodies plunging round them
falling round them on the white cold –
and somehow they're still aloft.

Is it my eyes
or are they at ease
in their bodies?
Hurling now at the narrower end
thirsty
          wanting hot whipped chocolate
expecting it to be there –
and it is there
          on the table.

They drink
          unsurprised
          do not blink.

MIRIAM SWIMMING

This is the brother she must push away
through the water to the tall reeds. She lowers
him, then herself, down into the river. Her hair
trails, she can feel its own dark weight
upon the surface. The basket breathes
inside its thick, rough-sculpted pitch.
The boy is quiet, as if he knew she'd have to push
him under were he to make a cry. Because
the cry of a boy child would change everything,
even what has gone before. Even the meaning
of the first garden, whose closed gates
would sag, whose angels falter for a moment
on their guard, if they did not already know
her feet in the water, her terrified rebellion.

She was afraid of water. It took me years
to lift her down, to have her come gladly
to this treated pool. We are numbered here.
We have slipped over on the tiles, and now we
lie half-satisfied among the artificial waves,
the fountains, ignoring when we can the dusty
rubber plants, the warts, verrucas we could catch.
These are the public baths, their minor penalties.
She dreams far backwards in her rubber ring
as though she's somewhere water's not confined,
as though the tiles on the walls had opened
and on the tarmac there's an angel, waiting
with his remote, un-Leisure Centred mind
towards whom she drifts, waves, opens her hand.

DAUGHTERS AT THE LAKE

My daughter is six.
She swims like a collie dog
hands smacking the ruffled surface
neck strained backwards

blonde tentacles of milfoil reach towards her
but her head outgolds them.
She makes a clear path through the weed

I cannot celebrate this simply.
I have never loved like this.

Sunheat warms my swollen belly
big with the next one.
I can hear the beaver's tail
against the water
its sharp handclap of praise

Elsewhere I know there stands a woman
big-bellied also, but not with tilth
who bends beside a brown lake, hungering.
She too has never loved like this

She is not my shadow, my black side;
she lives

As with my wet tongue
I moisten my lips
so she spits on her fingers
to moisten the mouth of her child.

There is no synchrony here
no balanced dance of continents
only the ragged flapping rhythms
of impure water in a human world

I lift my eyes.
Two whirring blurs of color
hang in the air:
hummingbirds sucking the nectar
that is still there.

'WHAT CAN WE SELL EXCEPT PARTS OF OURSELVES?' *Sonja Besford*

I did not exactly sell you. I left
you there in the woods of your own free will,
you with your dog, my daughter, running swift

around the house, untroubled by the heft
of my thought-basket stumbling up the hill.
I did not exactly sell you. I left

before I could know what it was I left,
or that my thought-basket would soon be full
of you with your dog, my daughter, running swift

around the little house, the place I left
because of some ache I could not name. Still
I did not exactly sell you. I left

you with your father knowing you'd be safe
but not that I could not be sound. Will
you with your dog, my daughter, running swift

come back to me, unanchored, lost, adrift,
if I can make a home to keep us whole?
I did not exactly sell you. I left
you with your dog, my daughter, running swift.

GHOST MILK

When I walked in Regents Park feeding the squirrels
and ducks, a goose pulled at my coat. I felt that ache,
that sting in my breasts that I felt with my children
before I had to leave them. Why do the feelings crouch
inside? I got my girls away, safe from the ovens.
So why does the ghost milk return, making me ache
with nothing but a white goose pulling me back
with her beak?

THE DARK AGES: ARTEFACTS

GLASS CLAW BEAKER

I wrestle with what this is:
green glass, thick,
rough goblet shaped
lined and ringed around the rim
for a rough gob
with handles like bulbs
or horses' arses
split by a plaited blue glass tail

green buttocks hooping out
a perfect resting place for fingers –
cup that bulges
so it makes a cup
of the hand
so a host can say
Have a hollow in your palm.
Drink. Press your claws
in these glass plaited flanks
tonight, for peace's sake.

CHESSLE DOWN BROOCH

A bridal gift? Stern swirls
of silver gilt to keep her
buckled. 'My lord, what loveliness is here!'
She feels the upraised tendrils
on gilded metal, figures
what she's worth.
'I am your servant my lord.
Have grace to those whose lives
you hold in balance.'
He bends to plant his lips upon her neck.

She hates her mother now
who unclasped her
to make this rough alliance,
weaving peace with her body.
She hangs on his shoulder
hopes to be held.

HELMET MADE OF IRON

Was it heavy on you, boy, this head upon your head?
What colour were your eyebrows
beneath the textured silvered bronze?
The metal mouth looks gold – it's only tin.
Did your lips sweat under it?

Only the eyes are hollow
A soldier has to see to fight.
What does he see?
A woman yelling 'I can't get near you
man with iron skin. Where do you hurt?'
coming at him with her claws
going for his eyes.

GOLD BUCKLE WITH NIELLO INLAY

He pulls me tight round his waist
inserts my one gold tooth
into its leather hole.
His belly overhangs me
so I dig in.
He relieves himself with a finger
behind my beaten lacework.

I can hear his gut working overtime.
He wants to unnotch me, fling me in a heap
but they're all looking at him in the hall.
He must fill his gob once more,
not show he has a pain
wants to lie down, be mothered.
I am a hero's buckle
a kind of burr that sticks.

WHALEBONE CASKET

The things they made from whales!
Corsets to keep a girl from spilling over,
make her *stay*,
and this eighth century half-caste thing
half runic and half Roman
where boars in heat stand out
against a carved cross, Christ
doles blessing down to trees
and soldiers scour the sky for – what?
Who is the hero of this piece?
The carver made it so it swung both ways.
When what's inside's too dear to lose
– what was it? Jewels? A child's bones? –
you have to get the spelling right,
carve it so it spans two worlds
and hope one picture holds
the password that will push the relics
out of this world, into the one that's coming next.

ONE OF A PAIR OF GOLD SHOULDER CLASPS

When dress was just a rough cloth circle
wrapped round the body, cut to size and sewn,
one single seam, with whalebone needles,
this shoulder clasp was one of two
to hold the clothing steady.
What lay beneath, next to the skin?
A leather vest perhaps, something smooth
to cool the itch, the sweating chafe of wool –

so when she pulls the thin gold chain
hooked to the pin that locks both halves
and puts her hand upon the hairs
between his breasts, or looses her own clasp
to free her nipple so the child can suck –
whatever the occasion, feed or fuck,
the necessary ornament's laid by
to glint on a sun topped table for an hour
then drop down in the dust –

That clasp on the museum shelf,
is it the one she kept, or lost?

ON NOT ADMIRING ANOTHER'S GIFTS

Yes, I can see the man has the habit of ease about him,
the way the sky breaks
like stalks around his back
while he twists wire round the rambler
so it will pour over the little wall

the way, under his hand, the flea-ridden cat
submits to be dipped, itching less already
as it yowls out of its grey water
drenched and weasel-smooth

and the air through the mirror
is solid round his shoulders,
substance of air, not thin
gravid almost, if air could be.

I can see all this
and surely, surely it is good.

I had a dream, rolled out
so long it seemed to stretch
like plastic cloth laid down
by a midwife for catching blood
right to the last wooden quiet
and piped music of the undertaker's hall.

And all along the cloth, a voice, my own, called out
Don't go. Wait for me. Stay.

But such a little voice.
Not mine, surely. Surely not.
And wrapped around the voice, feelings
that lived in things once known:
an empty cupboard,
a felt toy's beckoning, upraised arm, unanswered.

The cloth thinned, then, in my dream,
effacing back to nothing, to words,
a kind of nothing. It all turns abstract,
and I start to bed down in the safety of that old hole,
understanding. *This was not mine*
chimes out my other voice. *Really,
it was just an idea. Take it. Do!*

The little one can still throw a tantrum.
Sometimes I hear *Don't go.*

*I'll slam your fingers in the gate
if you go.* But it is so soft
so made dead by sand
and understanding that she weeps
in corners, mouth held tight
to not be heard.

Such a weight of knowing
round me – *Of course I understand.
Yes, you must go. I quite see –*
that even the air, compliant as it is
will not open its opportunities
for my arms to cut through,
the cat leaps from my hand,
the sky will not bend
to my desire.

Of course I understand.

WHEN IN THE EARLY HOURS

When in the early hours you reach
your arm down round my waist

when in the first sharp light of morning
I feel your teeth upon my neck

then I know that I will eat again
the fierce feast spread for me:

nectar from the bear's thick padded paws
honey from the curved claw of the bear.

BEING ALIVE

Friends die close to us. Our own deaths live
in our fingers   even now while your hands
hold me still for love.   I am dreaming

past the woman bent above the
cutting table   scissors flying across
the cloth

       My wall dissolves
as the future gives in desire
as the woman opens to take
the man.

How is conception made?

Ball of cells lodged
in the wall of the womb

splitting   splitting

nucleus daring itself
further into complexity
until the neck of the womb folds

back to let the child down a corridor
of bones pressed against the body's lips
and out to breathe

this air that is not
pure but all
there is for us to
breathe

HIGH WINDS

The wind is high so often now
I can smell the sea
churning up the river
like a judge who says
I come.

Has My Lady turned utterly against us?
Have we sucked her out
and delved our fingers in her secret places
till we are past forgiveness?

Or is there a Mother's hand in this?
Of One who says
You imagined you could destroy it all,
child?

Be still.
And listen to my breath
upon your broken banks,
your proud sea wall.

AIR PLANTS

These plants can live on nothing, says the blurb.
They draw their nutrients and their moisture from the air.
The women queue, curious to see what kind of thing
fulfils its needs immaculately. (The pale green tufty leaves
sit tight inside a shell or on a log of wood.) Like Princess Di,
who never seems to eat the piece of chicken
in her fingers. She holds it while she speaks.
At last she puts it down. And smiles,
without a bite, on and on,
at the Premature Babies Unit Charity Do.
If *they* can live on nothing
why can't you?

ADJUSTMENT

I saw myself as Andromache
      with Hector dead
I dreamed I held my daughter
while a foolish Greek
a drunken victor
mocking, said

Madam, you must let her go
down that steep crevasse.
Drop her now and come along
with me. Come back to Greece.

I dreamed I smiled
and spat on him.
The words of any true-born
Trojan woman
      fell from my tongue
If she goes
      I go
I'll rob you of
      those tedious tears
      that wordy tragedy
      called by my name…

THE TOWER (II)
by Julia Casterton and Chris Nawrat

I memorised a thousand sacred poems
and then forgot them

entered a walled garden,
made it a desert.

Prayed. Begged the voice to come.
'I have done without food,

without honey or milk.
I am waiting.

Only say the word.'
The voice came.

'The language of grace
lies hidden. Only accidence

can find it. Fasting is no use,
nor is excess.

There are some words
for whom the molecules of the air move

in the same dance
they dance for the thing that stands there.

House. Perhaps the air dances around that word
just as it dances round the house itself.

Or it may not be house.
Perhaps it is house in another language

that makes the dance. Or perhaps
that language is not yet spoken. Or heard.

There were towns where the people could not travel
without first learning another tongue.

The language of confusion had overgrown
what remained

of the language of grace.
But children, moving between the towns,

began to speak in their own words
in no language at all

in the simplex that lies

beneath the tower of contention.
When you discover those towns

be silent. Listen to the children
travelling from place to place.

Listen to what they do not yet
know how to say. Perhaps the word

is beginning. Or ending.
I can't be sure. I have forgotten.

Perhaps, words are only there for comfort
and the rest is nothing, only bliss.

And words exist for when
we cannot hear the bliss.'

October 23 1997

VOICES OF THINGS

Is there a vase that does not want to be held
that does not want to be filled with water running
from a tap, daffodils, ferns, baby's breath
by your hands?
      A cotton sweatshirt not waiting
to be pulled over your head and hang upon
your shoulders?
      A cup that does not long for your lips
to drink from it?
      Leather shoes, unlaced,
tongues at bay, for your feet to live in,
and the carpet for when your feet emerge,
heels, toes, deep in its sullen colours?
The air broken through by your body
moving in the night?

And yet the world does not want you,
you know this, you are sure
because one particular voice, the only voice,
has put you on hold for two impossible weeks
and will not, however many times you press Playback,
reveal herself on your
answering machine.

THE FALLING IN LOVE WORKSHOP

I am leading you
one by one
into a warm room.

You are naked except for the scarf that binds
                                        your eyes.

You are thinking about yourself,
of your longing to be touched
heard
taken into someone's eyes
mouth
other mouth

You are warm.
No one touches you and the longing grows.
Longing aches from your capillaries, from your hairs,
your breath.

Only one person can give you what you need.

You are lying down. You lie
on the soft carpets in the room.
You open your arms. You stretch them.
They meet one other body. Your breathing
rises in hope. You are in pain
with hope.
            Now I am removing the bandages.

Look!
You open your eyes
and begin to be in love.

You can do this with anyone,
almost anyone at all.

WHAT I REALLY WANTED TO SAY WAS

there are no words.
Only the body's silence
its ache, its sudden light

on the garden with its ghosts.
Death lies in the flesh
a hidden bud.

I look at the child's skin –
scarred, perfect,
her own death inscribed already

upon the cells.
I need to know this
inside, with my body's knowing –

this hand, that I hold to cross a road
is only now. Beyond
the dreams of language

filled with what's gone
or to come.
Times that matter, but that depend

on your hand: scarred, perfect,
held in my body's knowing
as we cross a road

my daughter.

THIRTEEN POEMS IN THE PERFUMED GARDEN
FOR THE SOUL'S RECREATION

'And after the enjoyment is over, and your amorous struggle has come to an end, be careful not to get up at once, but withdraw your member cautiously. Remain close to the woman, and lie down on the right side of the bed that witnessed your enjoyment. You will find this pleasant, and you will not be like a fellow who mounts the woman after the fashion of a mule, without any regard to refinement, and who, after the emission, hastens to get his member out and to rise. Avoid such manner, for they rob the woman of all her lasting delight.'

'And after the enjoyment is over...'

what else is there to do but look at the moon?
We are empty, as the moon is empty,
as we made her empty since we walked on her.

We are full, as the moon is full,
full of ourselves, the gift we have just given away,
unaware that we are walked on

or that plenitude is frowned upon. We are full, now,
and though desire will return, making us full
with emptiness again, just for now we are looking at the moon

who is unaware that she was walked on,
or, if she knows, she doesn't care,
or she has forgiven the spacemen
if she could be bothered to forgive.

'...and your amorous struggle has come to an end...'

Remember the years when you were sharkmeat,
when builders would call insults at you
because they liked the look of your little tits
and big arse, and walking down the road

was running a gauntlet of pitchforks,
nerves flayed, sweat dripping from your fingers?
Remember the chat-ups, where boys or older men
made sure they'd undermined all your beliefs,

even the small one you had in yourself
before the sex that left you unsatisfied,
you thinking it was all your own fault?
Well, that's all over now,

you're free of the wicked teeth kept, or not kept, pearly white.
When you cross the street now nobody sees you
except the friend with the eyes of love
who waits to greet you on the pavement

lips open with a memory of delight,
eyes with their expectations of delight.

'...be careful not to get up at once...'

because the day is out there with its absurd demands –
the news, the crowds of people shouting at their mobile phones,
the importunate. All want money
which you lack, and if you continue lying here
and don't open the blinds, the world easily forgets,
at least for a while, that you exist
and you can wrap yourself again
around your lover's sleeping body,
hold his feet in your hands
and feel the nerves, alive from dreams,
leaping in the hollows of your palms
and the ease your hands can bring to his feet
if you stay still and hold them just a little longer.

'...but withdraw your member cautiously...'

into the holy air of this room,
air that's steeped in the scent of our bodies,
whose dust is us, or was us till it fell from us
and now fills the air with the floating lights
we recognise as belonging both to ourselves and to the world,
our extensions, making self-love into love of the world
which greets your member now
as you withdraw it cautiously from the inside of me.

'Remain close to the woman...'

Or not. Now, it's not necessary to stay close
as it was when I was young and full of fear.

Now, take your own space as you need it.
The world is yours, as it is also mine.

'and lie down on the right side of the bed...'

So that your heart stays open, and uncongested
with the blood of memories. Let your ears
hear the noises outside in the common garden –

our family of frogs, the wood pigeons with their sighing,
but most of all the blackbird,
who knows more than we do about gratitude.

'You will find this pleasant...'

as you do any moment where you've drunk your fill
of what you need. There may not be long
before desire kicks in again, with its steel-tipped boots,
but before it does, what difference is there
between us and the gods?
Surely in those moments we are the gods.

'and you will not be like a fellow who mounts the woman after the fashion of a mule...'

though there was time when, like that other bewitched queen,
all I saw were asses. At parties,
I'd be the woman who fell for the man
who proclaimed that we fart, on average,
fourteen times a day. Why?
Why did I fall for them?

Because they were fools who made no claim,
I could dote on them, pity them, make excuses
for their cruelty. They were only asses after all.
A fellow who mounts a woman after the fashion of a mule
would have been far too fearsome.

Asses were easy. Something to fawn on
while waiting for the return of Oberon.

'without any regard for refinement...'

and sometimes, when the moon rises
full over Cable Street, refinement is the last thing
my body needs. The love parade has passed.
There's only this furious need
for desire to be over.
Any mule will do at those times.

'...after the emission...'

This is the mysterious time
that capitalism knows nothing whatever about.
Drunk. Satisfied.
After all the capture and rapture
this is what we came for.
Is is enough? Can we hold ourselves here
needing nothing
for just a few moments longer?

'...hastens to get his member out and to rise...'

Rise if you want. We've lived long enough
to know there's no spurning in this.
It only means you need to stand, stretch,
Walk to the kitchen for something.

I'll stay here, in the bed.
Sex is still with me,
the doorway we walked through,
the room where we forgot who we were

and so became the world and all her creatures, the world with her moon.

'Avoid such manners...'

The manners I'd like you to avoid are these:
there are really none. I'd like you to do,
exactly, as you please.
And I will do as I please too.

'For they rob the woman of all her lasting delight.'

None can rob me of that now,
Though I think one tried in the past,
one who felt so short himself
he had to steal from others.

Now, I can close my eyes and there's the garden.
We were never thrown out. How could we be?
The garden is always growing, always perfecting itself
with snakes and trees and knowledge everywhere

for us to eat and talk to. And the god,
walking around and causing trouble, lording it,
even he can't ruin things.

LIST OF SUBSCRIBERS

A G Adair
Anna Adams
Victoria Adderley
Shahab Ahmed
Stephanie Allen-Early
Liz Almond
Ambit
Susan Aspell
Margaret Aspinall
Fay Avsec
Allan E Baker
Helene Baker
Chrissy Banks
Elspeth Barker
Barbara Barnes
Celia Barry
Martin and Judy Bax
Rosi Beech
Rosalind Beeton
Judi Benson
Anne Berkeley
Sonja Besford
Clare Best
Margaret Beston
J. Louise Bibby
Elizabeth Birchall
Hamish Stuart Black
Anne Born
Sarah Braun
Elizabeth Brock and Fred Wolf
Felicity Brookesmith
Paula Brown and Stephen Brennan
Alan Brownjohn
Alan Burton
A W J Burton
Maggie Butt
Mark Carson
Mavis Carter
Marjorie Carter
Sarah Cave
Duncan Chambers
Linda Chase
V E Chisholm
Valerie Clarke
Polly Clarke
Robert Cole and Susie Reynolds
Anthony Coleman
Roy Collins
George Coppen
Jane Corbett
Martina Cotter
Niall Craig
Katherine Crocker
Angela Croft
Simon Currie
Andrew da Silva

Emma Danes
Doris Dembosky
Josephine Dickinson
Brian Docherty
Chris Dodd
Tom Duddy
Christina Dunhill
Alyss Dye
Margaret Eddershaw
Gillian Elinor
Fred Ellis
Tammy Evans
Erica Facey
Janet Fisher
Mary Franklin
Jane Fraser Esson
Tony Frazer
Leah Fritz
Judy Gahagan
Donald Gardner
Peter Gilmour
Chrissie Gittins
Peter Godfrey
Joyce Goldstein
Harriet Grace
Jan Grant
John Green
David Harmer
Ted Harriott
Jo Haslam
P D Havercroft
Jean Hayes
Rosanna Hibbert
Jill Higgins
Jemma Hill
Sheila Hillier
Anthony Hills
Theresa Hind
Lynne Hjelmgaard
Sophy Hoare
Kathy Hobson
Penny Hodgkinson
Peter Howard
Sue Hughes
Naomi Jaffa
Helen Jagger Wood
Bruce John James
Roy Jeffs
Maureen Jivani
Peter Johnson
Judith Kazantzis
Cathy Keable-Elliott
Pauline Keith
Andrew Kelly
Mimi Khalvati
Jenny King
Richard King
Angela Kirby

Wendy Klein
Karen Knight
Joel Lane
Doris Louisa Lampard
Tess Lancashire
Janet Lancaster
Keith Lander
Bernard Landreth
Michael Laskey
Francesca Latella
Gill Learner
Michael Lee
Howard Lester
Maureen Li
Ofra Livay
Louise A. Logue
Herbert Lomas
Helen Lovelock-Burke
Janet Loverseed
Tony Lucas
Barbara Ludman
Anna Lynch
Gwen MacKeith
Ivana Mackinnon
Roohi Majid
Lorraine Mariner
Jehane Markham
Antoinette Marshall
John Marshall
David Martyn
Nancy Mattson and
        Michael Bartholomew-Biggs
Robin Maunsell
Tim May
Diana McCleary
Dorothy McCuller
Celia McCulloch
Lucie McKee
Stuart McKenzie
Tony McKeown
Doreen McPherson
Mary Michaels
Adrian Mitchell
Jeremy Moore
Christopher Morgan
Claire Morgan
Charles William Morgan M.B.E.
Barbara A Morton
Madeline Munro
Katrina Naomi
Caroline Natzler
Chris Nawrat
Helena Nelson
Rosemary Norman
Henry O'Connor
William Palmer
Luigia Parkinson
Joyce Anora Patterson

Viv Pegram
Kate Pemberton and Daniel MacDonald
Margaret Perry
J M Pestel
Peter Phillips
Keith Please
The Poetry Business
Katrina Porteous
Rosalynde Price
Mel Pryor
Ian Purser
The Rialto
Jessica Robinson
Sylvia Rowbottom
Marion Ryder
Carole Satyamurti
Kate Scott
Cecilia Scurfield
Desmond Sequeira
Marian Shaw
Rosie Shepperd
Joan Sheridan Smith
The SHop
Margaret Slater
Bill Smith
Sheila Smith
Penny Solomons
Ellen Spiring
Norman Staines
Anne Stewarts
Alicia Stubbersfield
Lizzi Thistlethwayte
Wisty Thomas
Martina Thomson
Samuel Tongue
Tabby
Joseph Turrent
Selwyn Veater
Karina Vidler
John and Hilary Wakeman
Michelene Wandor
Roger Waterfield
Rosalind Waterman
Rita Watts
Derek Webster
Rywa Weinberg
Jane Wibberley
John Williams
Roddy Williams
Sarah Williams
Emily Wills
Anthony Wilson
Peter Wilson
Francesca Wolf
Marguerite Wood

And other subscribers who wish to
remain anonymous.